Many Ways to Work

Abby Jackson

Contents

Rigby®

A Harcourt Achieve Imprint

www.Rigby.com
1-800-531-5015

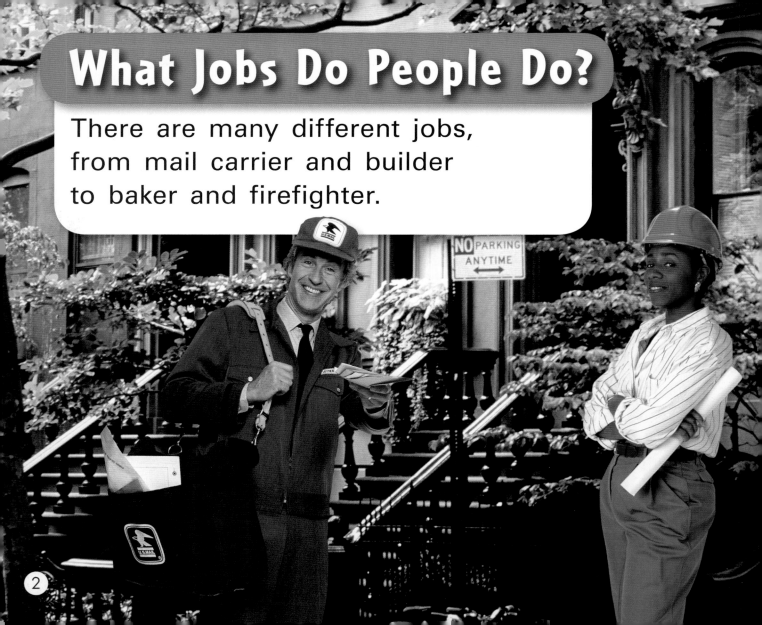

What Jobs Do People Do?

There are many different jobs, from mail carrier and builder to baker and firefighter.

Some of these people grow
or make things to sell.
They work with **goods**.

Other people teach you, help you,
and keep your **community** safe.
They work with **services**.

3

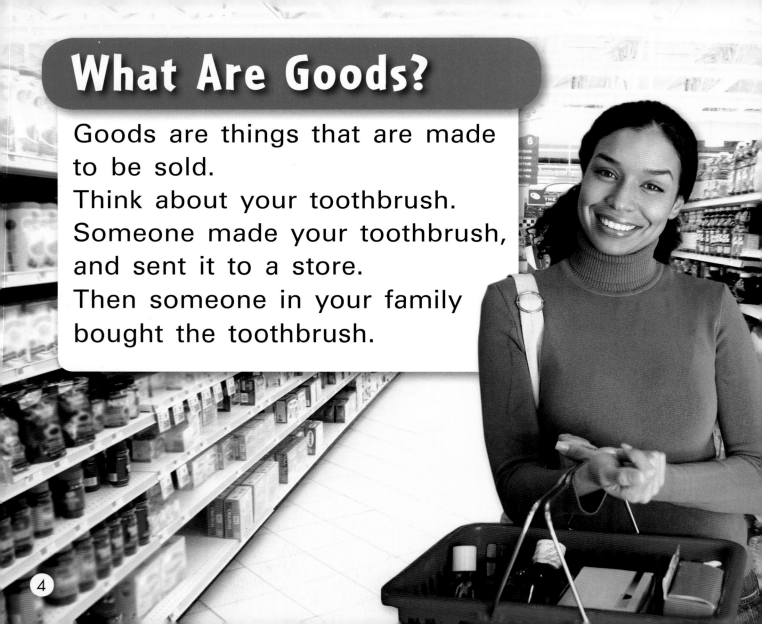

What Are Goods?

Goods are things that are made to be sold.
Think about your toothbrush. Someone made your toothbrush, and sent it to a store.
Then someone in your family bought the toothbrush.

Now you use it to brush
your teeth.
Your toothbrush is
a kind of *good*.

Where Do Goods Come From?

Some goods, such as fruit, are grown.
Other goods, such as cakes and clothes, are made.

Oranges grow on trees
on large farms.
Farmers care for the trees
and pick the fruit when
it is ready.
The fruit is then sold
at markets.

Many people still make clothes by hand.
But most clothes are made in a **factory**.
Machines **weave** and sew the cloth.
More clothes can be made in less time.

Bakers work in large kitchens.
They use eggs, sugar,
and flour to make
cookies, breads, and cakes.
These treats are then sold
at stores or restaurants.

What Are Services?

A service is another kind of work.
Think again about your toothbrush.
What else do you need
to take care of your teeth?

You need to go to
the dentist.
The dentist helps
keep your teeth
clean and healthy.
The work she does
is a *service*.

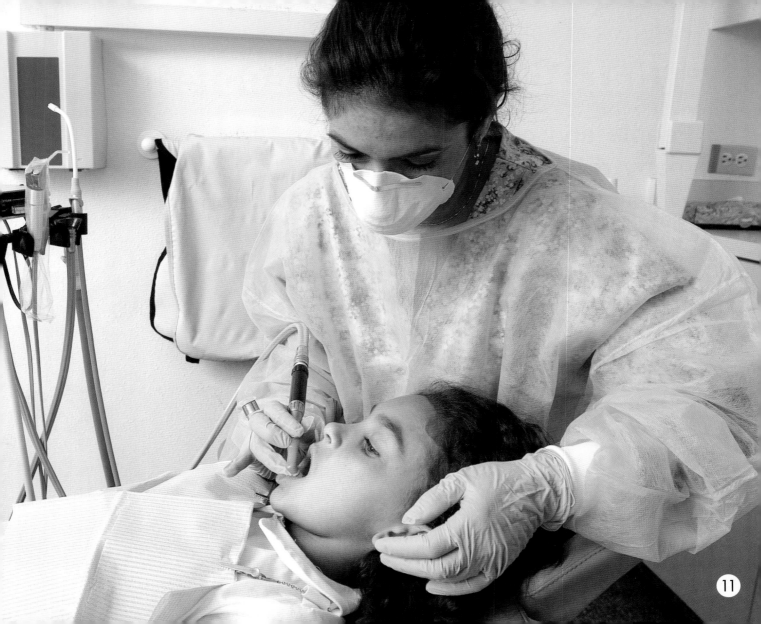

What Services Do People Need?

People and communities need
many different services.
We all need teachers and other people
to help keep us safe and healthy.

Teachers **provide** a very important service.
They help us learn to read, write, and think.
Teachers also help us learn to play sports, dance, and make art!

Police and firefighters keep us and our homes safe from harm. Doctors, nurses, and dentists keep our bodies strong.

Some people make goods to sell.
Other people do things to help people.

What kind of work do you want to do?

Glossary

community a group of people who live or work together

factory a large building in which things are made to be sold

goods things that are made to be sold

provide to give people something they need

services work someone does for money

weave to bring threads together to make cloth